ITCH!

Everything You Didn't Want to Know About What Makes You Scratch

by Anita Sanchez
illustrated by Gilbert Ford

Houghton Mifflin Harcourt • Boston • New York

For Dutchess, Liza, Sam, Corey, Jessie, Franklin,
and many other furry companions. —A.S.

Text copyright © 2018 by Anita Sanchez
Illustrations copyright © 2018 by Gilbert Ford

hmhco.com

The text of this book is set in Egyptienne and Regula.

Library of Congress Cataloging-in-Publication Data is on file.
ISBN 978-0-544-81101-0

Manufactured in China
SCP 10 9 8 7 6 5 4 3 2 1
4500689912

Contents

CHAPTER ONE

SKIN!

A Bag with You Inside

Everything you are—all your thoughts, dreams, fears—every breath you take—your heart, your brain, your blood—it's all contained inside your skin. But you probably never give skin a thought—until it gets itchy.

Skin is like a bag holding you together. But it isn't like a plastic bag, airtight and waterproof. Things can get on, or under, or into your skin, and can give you a big ITCH.

Your skin isn't the same all over. On top of your head, it grows lots of hair. On your palms, there's no hair at all. Your skin is paper-thin and delicate around your eyes, much thicker on the bottom of your feet. So some parts of it are more likely to get itchy. That's why wool socks might be annoying on the sensitive skin of your ankles but not bother the tough soles of your feet.

If you could somehow peel off your skin and spread it on the floor, it would cover about twenty square feet—the size of a blanket on a double bed. Your skin is your body's largest organ. And like all of your body's organs, it has a crucial job to do.

You can feel your heart pumping blood around your veins while your lungs breathe air in and out. It may seem as though your skin just sits there under your clothes, not doing much. But it is working hard every minute of every day. It helps protect you from danger—germs, burns, frostbite.

Your skin stretches and grows. Air and water can flow through it. When damaged, it can (usually) repair itself. And it comes in many beautiful colors.

A TRIPLE-DECKER SANDWICH

Your skin is made up of three layers:

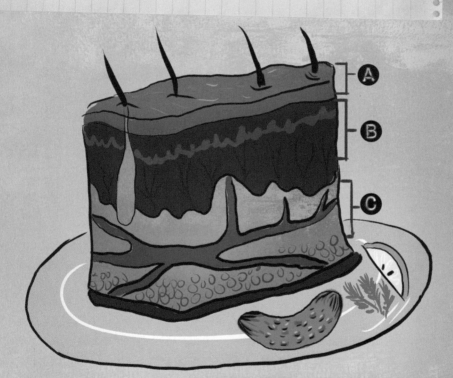

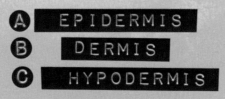

- Ⓐ EPIDERMIS
- Ⓑ DERMIS
- Ⓒ HYPODERMIS

Epidermis

The topmost part—the part you see and touch—is not living tissue. It's made up of skin cells that have died. These cells flake off a little at a time. In fact, you are constantly shedding your entire skin, speck by speck. When you vacuum up the dust under your bed, a lot of it is you.

Other creatures also shed their epidermis. Furry mammals such as bears or mice shed epidermal cells the way we do, a flake at a time. Some animals shed their skin all in one piece. Snakes, for example, wriggle and rub against things until the outer layer of skin loosens. Even the skin over their eyeballs peels off. The snake slithers away in its glossy new skin, leaving the dead skin behind like a dry, rustling ghost. Imagine if humans did that!

Underneath the dead skin cells is the epidermis: living skin that's constantly at work. It creates new skin cells, which work their way upward. It takes only a few weeks for them to reach the top layer and flake off. Your epidermis creates a whole new skin for you every month or so.

Dermis

This skin layer is like a factory, cranking out many products. The dermis makes the hairs that sprout on your head, arms, and other parts of your body. It creates oil that keeps your skin healthy and supple. And it oozes sweat, which cools you when it evaporates.

The dermis also contains blood vessels that bring nutrients and oxygen to the skin and carry away waste. Nerve endings are located there, too.

Hypodermis

The innermost layer of skin is mostly a padding of fat, which protects your muscles and bones from bumps. Fat is good insulation, so it helps keep you from getting too hot or too cold.

Glance at the skin on the back of your hand. Doesn't look like there's much going on there. But in one square inch of skin, there are about 500 sweat glands, 20 blood vessels, and 1,000 nerve endings. These nerves are incredibly sensitive: they let you feel a snowflake, a warm breeze—or a mosquito bite.

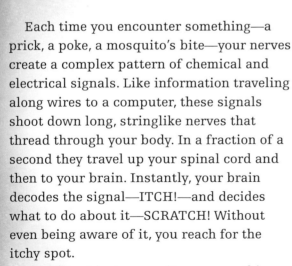

SWEAT GLANDS   BLOOD VESSELS   NERVE ENDINGS

Each time you encounter something—a prick, a poke, a mosquito's bite—your nerves create a complex pattern of chemical and electrical signals. Like information traveling along wires to a computer, these signals shoot down long, stringlike nerves that thread through your body. In a fraction of a second they travel up your spinal cord and then to your brain. Instantly, your brain decodes the signal—ITCH!—and decides what to do about it—SCRATCH! Without even being aware of it, you reach for the itchy spot.

Yet it's not just mosquitoes; many things can make your skin itchy. But here's the question—WHY?

Soothe the Itch:

THE ITCH-SCRATCH CYCLE

The Center for the Study of Itch: it's a real place, a laboratory at Washington University in St. Louis. Scientists there have discovered a frustrating fact: the more you scratch, the more you itch! Scratching causes only very mild pain, but it's enough to trigger pain receptors in the brain, which release a chemical called serotonin. Serotonin soothes pain—but causes itchiness.

If you're scratching without realizing it, clip your fingernails very short. Rub the itchy area with your fingertips instead of scratching with your nails.

So Sorry, Didn't Mean to Irritate You

Some of the most irritating villains in nature don't mean to make you itch! Fleas, bedbugs, mosquitoes, poison ivy, and lice—believe it or not, it's just a coincidence that most humans have allergic reactions to them.

Most insect bites and poison ivy rashes don't start itching instantly. It can take hours, or even days, for the itching to begin. This lag time between contact and itch is a clue that the itching is an accidental byproduct.

Itchy Bug Spit

Some insects, such as mosquitoes or bedbugs, bite you in order to suck your blood for food. Seems as if that would mean a big OUCH! But the insect spits some of its saliva into your skin, and the saliva contains an anesthetic—a chemical that helps to lessen pain.

Usually blood clots, or thickens, soon after it's exposed to air. But insect spit also has anticoagulants, chemicals that keep the blood flowing smoothly.

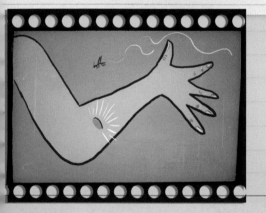

When a bug is done feasting on you, some saliva remains in your skin. This saliva is an allergen, a substance that causes an allergic reaction. The unfamiliar chemicals in this tiny bit of spit send a message to your body—fight off the invader! Your immune system kicks into action—unfortunately, too much action.

Sometimes your body's immune system is too "suspicious." To battle the intruder, your body creates a powerful chemical called histamine, which makes small veins in your skin swell up in the area around the bite. In the widened veins, lots of blood cells and proteins can rush to the danger zone to fight the problem. It's as though, after a traffic accident, there was only a narrow road for ambulances to get in—and then you suddenly widened the highway. All this extra blood produces a sensitive, itchy bump.

But it's not that bug saliva is a real threat—your immune system is overreacting.

histamine

Blood cells rush to danger, causing swelling

PICTURE START

Leave Me Alone!

So is all itching just a big mistake? Or do some plants and animals irritate us for a reason?

Itching can be a form of communication. A lion or bear just has to show their fangs and roar—and we'll stop bothering them! But for smaller, quieter creatures—caterpillars, for example—sometimes making enemies itchy is the best defense. Some itch-causing plants and animals are letting us know, clear as a lion's roar, *Leave me alone or I'll make you sorry!*

In these pages, you'll meet some of the creepiest, most annoying, and most downright irritating animals and plants on earth. But all of these organisms have one thing in common—they're really, really good at using the ITCH to survive!

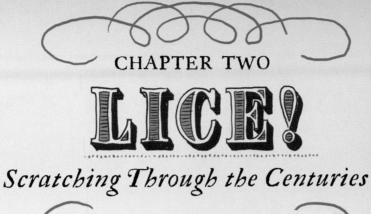

CHAPTER TWO

LICE!

Scratching Through the Centuries

France, 1918

A young soldier crouches in a muddy trench. Sleet drizzles on his helmet, and his toes are freezing. He's hungry and cold, but he can't rest—he has to keep a sharp eye out for German snipers. Every now and then a bullet zings past his head.

But almost worse than the risk of enemy fire is the tormenting itch all over his skin. He can feel tiny insects scurrying over his back and traveling through his hair. The soldier reaches underneath his helmet and captures a hair louse between his fingers. But the hard, slippery creature wriggles away before he can squash it. He doesn't even try to grasp the body lice—they dart away, hiding in his sleeves and underwear.

He's been wearing the same uniform for weeks now. It's always cold in the damp, filthy trenches, so he rarely even takes off his coat. Hundreds of lice eggs are glued to his hair, and more are buried in the seams of his shirt and trousers. The lice bite his skin many times each day, torturing him with a burning, intense itch that, like the war itself, never seems to stop.

* * *

Almost nothing creeps us out more than the thought of crawling, itchy lice. A louse is a small, wingless insect, about a third as big as a grain of rice. It has a small bite, but it packs a big ITCH.

This little creature has been causing humans itchy woes for a long time. Fossils show that lice have been around for more than a hundred million years. Neanderthals scratched lice bites on their hairy bodies more than fifty thousand years ago. These early humans had fuzzy hair all over, so there was lots of habitat available for hair lice. Then people started wearing clothing, and its seams and wrinkles created a whole new niche for body lice.

Archaeologists have found mummified lice in the hair of Egyptian Pharaohs. Rich and poor, male and female, young and old—humans have battled lice right up to today.

Lice spread quickly when there are a lot of people who are packed close together and don't have much opportunity to take baths and change their clothes. From ancient Romans to modern times, armies have been bugged by lice.

In World War I, soldiers often huddled shoulder to shoulder in trenches to avoid enemy bullets. Lice crawled from man to man. Soldiers called them "arithmetic bugs" because "they added to our woes, subtracted from our pleasures, divided our attention, and multiplied!" No matter if the soldiers were British, Russian, French, German, Turkish, or American, they all spent a lot of time miserably scratching louse bites.

But why do lice find humans so delicious?

Parasites are organisms that use other living things—like you and me—for food and shelter. Lice can die within hours if they're separated from the warmth and nutrition provided by their host.

Lice are host-specific parasites. There are several types of lice that live only on humans. There are also more than three thousand other kinds of lice, and each has its own host species. Bears get bear lice that clamber through thick fur. Birds get bird lice that lay eggs on feathers. Mice get very small lice.

Soothe the Itch:
YOU SCRATCH MY BACK AND I'LL SCRATCH YOURS

If you're itchy in a hard-to-reach spot, it's nice if someone helps out. Many animals spend lots of time scratching each other's itches. Horses stand side by side and nibble each other's backs with their teeth. Monkeys spend hours grooming each other, picking off lice—and eating them!

Even the biggest animals can be tormented by these tiny bugs. Horses have very sensitive skin that can sense the prick of a pin or a drop of rain. An elephant can feel a fly land on its back. Sometimes elephants bitten by lice scratch their backs so hard on a tree, they knock the tree over!

Soothe the Itch:
A DIRTY BATH?

People take baths with soap and water, but birds and mammals often take dirt baths, wallowing around in sand and dust. The gritty particles of soil scrub off lice and other parasites, and it must feel nice, like rubbing sandpaper on an itchy spot.

Water can also help animals wash off lice. Beavers and otters, which spend a lot of time swimming, have fewer lice than animals that never dive into the water.

A Lousy Life Cycle

Lice eggs are incubated by the body warmth of their host. It's only a matter of days before an egg hatches. A baby louse, called a nymph, crawls out of the shell and bites its host, sucking a droplet of blood. It keeps feeding, growing fatter and fatter. Soon it sheds its exoskeleton like a too-tight pair of jeans.

The nymph grows fast. In only about two weeks, it's ready to mate. A female can lay up to ten eggs a day. Soon new nymphs are grown, ready to lay eggs. Then their babies grow up and lay eggs, and so on—until thousands of lice could be crawling on the skin of their unwilling host.

LICE: INCOMPLETE METAMORPHOSIS

Egg–Nymph–Adult

egg   Nymph1   Nymph2   Nymph3   Adult

Host? Not Me!

Long ago, lice-infested soldiers longed to take baths and rid themselves of the itch. Today, showering can sometimes seem like a chore, but if you never bathed, your skin would suffer. Lice, fungi, and other parasites would flourish on your skin. In past centuries, keeping clean was a challenge, but nowadays, with indoor plumbing, showers, and washing machines, it's easier to keep lice away.

But even with modern shampoos and showers, lice are tough to get rid of. The little bugs are slippery and fast moving. Lice seem like slowpokes, though, compared with some of the animal kingdom's mightiest jumpers and their incredible acrobatics.

Avoid the Itch:
LICE ADVICE

If you don't want to host some six-legged guests, don't use anyone else's brush or comb, or wear someone else's clothes until you wash them in hot, soapy water. Louse eggs (called nits) can attach to hairs or stick to a hat or clothing.

If you do find out you're hosting lice, don't freak out! Hair lice don't spread disease or cause serious health problems. Still, you don't want insects using your head for a habitat. See your doctor to find out how to get rid of unwanted company. Body lice can carry germs—so they're a more serious health concern than hair lice.

actual size

CHAPTER THREE

FLEA!

Welcome to the Circus

New York City, 1957

Excited crowds flock to Professor Heckler's minuscule circus in Times Square. They're eager to see his famous acrobats balance on high wires and leap through the air.

But in this circus the performers are much, much smaller than the audience—so small that the audience uses magnifying glasses to see them. The performers are, in fact, insects.

Welcome to the flea circus! "You won't believe your eyes, and you'll be scratching your heads in amazement!" the ringmaster shouts. The audience crowds around a table as the performers jump and soar, bouncing off tiny trapezes and tightropes. Harnessed by a slender gold wire around their bodies, four fleas pull an enormous coach a hundred times their size. The audience is armed with back scratchers, which come in handy when one of the stars makes a leap onto someone's neck.

Flea circuses once were a popular part of fairs and sideshows. And the audience really was watching an amazing display of athletic ability. Fleas are some of the most successful and well-adapted creatures on the planet. They have to be, in order to survive.

No one loves fleas! Other organisms are constantly trying to avoid them—or kill them. So fleas need to be fast, strong, and agile. Relative to their body size, fleas are among the best jumpers of the animal world. They can leap more than a hundred times their own height. If a person could do that, you could hop over a fifty-story building!

For centuries, scientists wondered how these tiny insects could make such big leaps. But fleas move too fast for us to see; they can take off in a thousandth of a second. It wasn't until 2011 that scientists at Cambridge University in England used high-speed recording equipment to film flea jumps.

After filming more than fifty flea leaps and analyzing them on a computer, Dr. Gregory Sutton and other scientists are starting to figure out the mystery of flea acrobats. Fleas have pads of a rubbery protein called resilin attached to their legs. As the flea bends its leg, the resilin acts like a bow being bent, stretching and stretching . . . and then it suddenly releases, catapulting the flea upward like an arrow shot from a bowstring.

Dr. Sutton suggests that fleas could serve as models for

FLEA RESILIN

engineers designing robots that have to travel over rough terrain. "Insect jumping is incredibly precise and incredibly fast," he says. "If you could build a robot that could do that, it would be fantastic." Imagine a flealike robot leaping over the craters of Mars!

But fleas still have secrets. Scientists are trying to figure out the details of these amazing flea leaps. For example, no one yet knows exactly how fleas lock their "bowstrings" in place and then suddenly release them.

A Mouth Like a Needle

Fleas have sharp, thin mouthparts that can pierce skin. The adults feed only on blood and can't survive long if they are away from a warm body. Fortunately for them, their strong jumping legs let them leap easily from host to host. Unlike lice, fleas can switch from one kind of host to another. If your dog has fleas, you can't get rid of the fleas by getting rid of the dog. The fleas will just jump on your cat—or you!

Soothe the Itch:
THINK NONTOXIC

If your cat or dog is scratching a lot, check to see if it has fleas. If so, you'll need to bathe your pet and clean its bedding weekly. But many commercial anti-flea products contain highly toxic chemicals. Read the labels! Try the least toxic alternatives first.

- *Use flea sprays and shampoos made from natural ingredients such as peppermint oil or eucalyptus.*

- *Cider vinegar is something fleas hate! Use it as a bath rinse or for cleaning a pet's sleeping areas.*

- *Experiment with adding garlic or brewer's yeast to your pets' food—it makes their blood less tasty to fleas.*

Fleas lay eggs on the host's skin—lots of eggs! Just one busy mother flea can lay about twenty eggs a day. The round white eggs often drop off into the host's home or bedding. When the eggs hatch, the caterpillar-like larvae eat the grossest food ever: bits of dried skin and hair, and even the parent flea's droppings.

The larvae grow fast, nourished by the protein-rich droppings. Soon they're ready to pupate. When the adult emerges from the pupa case, it can leap onto a host within seconds.

FLEA
a complete METAMORPHOSIS

adult

pupa

larva

eggs

Avoid the Itch:
FLEA TRAP

Fleas are attracted to light and warmth, so place a desk lamp on the floor, fill a shallow dish with soapy water, and put the dish under the lamp. Hopping toward the light, the fleas may land in the dish. Adding soap breaks the surface tension of the water, making it harder for fleas to swim to safety. (Yes, fleas can swim!)

Since young fleas grow up in an animal's bedding, fleas are a big, itchy problem for animals that return to the same bed—pet dogs and cats, as well as mice, beavers, woodchucks, squirrels, or rats. Animals that don't sleep in the same place every night, such as apes or deer, don't tend to get fleas.

Soothe the Itch:
OIL YOUR DOG

If your dog has sore, itchy skin from fleabites, try coconut oil. This pleasant-smelling oil is packed with vitamins and nutrients to help heal sore skin. Massage it into your dog's skin, especially around the tummy—the dog will love it! When you get the oil on your hands, it nourishes your skin, too. Coconut oil is nontoxic, so it doesn't matter if your pet licks its fur afterward.

OIL
— of —

Fleas live all their adult life on someone else's skin. That's why they're so weirdly shaped. If you look at a flea from the side, it's broad and flat, but if you look head-on, it's narrow. This unusual shape lets it easily slip between hairs. And fleas' bodies are hard and slippery smooth, making them almost impossible to catch.

Fleas and lice can travel from place to place. But there are other irritating things out there, ones that don't jump around. Often we hardly notice them—they're quiet, and they don't move a whole lot. But keep a sharp eye out for organisms that are powerful, itch-causing—and green.

CHAPTER FOUR

PLANTS!

The Green World Fights Back

Australia, 1799

In the dry, dusty soil of the Australian outback, almost nothing grows. So some enterprising farmers began to experiment with an amazing new crop from America: the cactus called prickly pear.

Prickly pears grew easily, even in the desert, producing lots of sweet purple fruit. And the plant's prickliness made it a living fence for livestock. Seemed like the perfect crop for those hardworking farmers!

But things didn't go quite as expected. In fact, it was an environmental disaster. Because prickly pears are, well . . . prickly. They're all but impossible to weed out.

You might not think of plants as powerful warriors. Seems as though they just sit there, waiting to be eaten. But greenery has been fighting back against herbivores for millions of years—and plants have an enormous arsenal of weapons. Plants can poison and stab us. And they can make us itch!

Like all cacti, prickly pears are covered with spines. These big prickers are an obvious warning: Don't touch me! But prickly pears also have spines called glochids—so small they're easy to brush against without noticing. These wicked little glochids look as soft as fur, but if you could study them under a microscope, you'd see that each one is barbed like a fishhook. At the lightest touch, they embed themselves in your skin. As you try to scratch them loose, they work their way in deeper, causing an ever-growing itch.

Soothe the Itch:
GLUE THE PRICKLES

Prickly pear glochids are so small they're very hard to remove. But if they're left in your skin, they can cause infection. If you get spined by a prickly pear, don't scratch—that will only rub the spines in deeper. Use tweezers to pull out each glochid. Or pour a bit of nontoxic glue on the affected part of your skin, let it harden, and then gently pull it off. The spines will stick to the glue.

Prickly pear cacti sprawl across the earth like a pile of fat green dishes balanced on one another. Every time the pile collapses and a "dish" touches the ground, it takes root almost instantly. Across Australia, the newly introduced prickly pears began to spread like a virus.

Soon hundreds, then thousands, then millions of acres were covered by prickly pears. The spiny snarl, twenty feet high in places, made whole farms uninhabitable. Houses and barns were crushed beneath the weight of the cactus. In despair, many farmers gave up and fled the itchy "green hell."

Prickly pears aren't evil plants. In their native desert habitat, they're important for wildlife. The tangles of itchy prickles are a great place for birds to build nests, safe from predators. Tortoises, snakes, and lizards hide from the desert sun in the life-giving shade of the prickly pear. The fruits are eaten by quail, woodpeckers, jack-rabbits, deer—and people. Apache Indians have enjoyed juicy prickly pears for centuries, and the fruits are sold in markets and grocery stores all over the world today.

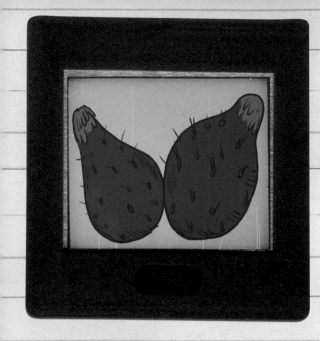

Avoid the Itch:
THORNY FRUIT

If you're brave enough to sample a prickly pear, chew carefully—glochids are found on the fruit's skin, and they can make your tongue, lips, and throat itch like crazy. The Apaches would roll the fruits in the desert sand to scour away the glochids. Wear gloves and scrub the fruit under running water to make sure the glochids are gone, and peel the fruit carefully.

Poison Ivy: A Tasty Treat

Poison ivy is another plant famous for making humans itch. It grows all over the place: forests, beaches, and backyards. Sometimes it creeps up a tree, reaching out its toxic leaves to brush your face. Sometimes it's low on the ground, just at ankle height.

The plant creates a sticky, oily chemical called urushiol, which is hidden beneath the surface of the leaves and bark. It protects the plant as if it were a liquid coat of armor. If you brush against poison ivy, the urushiol immediately oozes out and gets on your skin. If you're allergic, it can cause soreness, itching, and even big blisters.

But why? Why does poison ivy have it in for the human race?

28

Avoid the Itch:

POISON IVY, OAK, AND SUMAC

Poison ivy, poison oak, and poison sumac—these three plants are related, and all have the same toxic sap that can cause an epic rash and intense itchiness. Learning to identify these plants is the best way to steer clear of the itch.

Poison Oak — Poison Ivy — Poison Sumac

Actually, poison ivy isn't trying to make us itchy at all. It's targeting smaller enemies.

Plants have been fighting off insects for millions of years—long before humans were around. The thorns, poisons, and prickers of many plants evolved as a defense against the chewing mouthparts of insects and other herbivores—not humans. So poison ivy's urushiol is not aimed at you. Poison ivy is battling bugs.

When an insect bites a poison ivy leaf, the gooey, sticky urushiol flows out of the wound. It gums up the bug's jaws, stopping the bug from munching. Then the urushiol hardens and protects the injured leaf, like a scab on a cut finger.

Unfortunately, urushiol happens to be an allergen for most of us. About 85 percent of humans are allergic to it. A few are super-allergic to it, and a few people are completely immune. No one knows why some people are more sensitive than others.

But it's only humans who are so sensitive to this itchy chemical. In fact, many animals love to eat poison ivy. Goats are crazy about it, and sometimes flocks of goats are brought in to rid parks and yards of it. In the forest, woodpeckers feast on poison ivy berries, and moose and mice chew poison ivy leaves—and their mouths don't get itchy!

Soothe the Itch:
POISON IVY

A poison ivy rash usually lasts about three weeks. That's a long time to be itchy! To lessen the itch:

- *Give the rash air and sunlight; don't cover it with bandages.*
- *Take hot showers or oatmeal baths.*
- *Over-the-counter remedies such as witch hazel or calamine lotion help soothe the skin.*

If you happen to get a poison ivy rash, you don't have to hide from your friends! Poison ivy is not contagious.

Burdock: Spreading the Itch Around

Plants can't get up and run around. So some plants use irritation as a way to send their seeds traveling around the earth.

Burdock is a tall, floppy-leaved plant that originally grew in northern Asia, but now it's found all over the planet. No matter where you live—in the city, on a farm, north or south, east or west—likely there's a burdock in your yard or on the school grounds. That's because burdock is the world's best hitchhiker. It sticks to you like Velcro.

The plant is covered with round, prickly seedpods called burrs, with dozens of tiny barbed hooks. They grab anything that brushes against them—the feathers of a robin, the tail of a raccoon, your socks. Burrs often get tangled in dog fur. In fact, Velcro was invented by a scientist who got the idea while pulling burrs off his dog.

When a burr hitchhikes on you, you know it! The prickly hooks cause a bigtime ITCH. So you scratch. As the burr is torn apart by scratching, the seeds scatter far and wide. It's easy to imagine how burdocks have spread all around the globe, stuck in pant cuffs or animal tails.

Some plants can really be irritating, but at least they can't get up and chase us around. We can try to stay away from thorns and barbs that want to prick us. But it's almost impossible to escape from the whining flight of the world's most annoying insect . . .

CHAPTER FIVE

MOSQUITO!

Why They Love to Bite Us

EEEEEEEEEEEE. The high-pitched whine makes your ears itch even before you spot the little insect flying toward you. She wants to suck your blood!

The mosquito lands on your skin. Her six delicate legs tiptoe along your arm. Searching for a blood vessel, she pokes around with her long, tube-shaped mouth, called a proboscis. There it is—a handy vein.

Then she saws—yes, saws—a hole. Jagged mouthparts slice through the layers of skin and into the vein.

She steals less than a drop of your blood. But to a mosquito, that's a feast. Her blood-filled stomach stretches like a little red balloon. She flies away, leaving a hole in your skin that will soon begin to ITCH.

But why do mosquitoes love people? Why do they chase us around, whine in our ears, and risk getting slapped and squashed?

Mosquitoes feed on blood, but unlike fleas or lice, they don't do it because they're hungry. Most species of mosquitoes sip flower nectar for food. It's only females about to lay eggs that are bloodthirsty.

Blood is made up of proteins. Female mosquitoes need those proteins to make lots of eggs. They can produce a few eggs without a blood meal, but after a drink of your nutritious blood, a mother mosquito is an egg-producing machine. She can lay a hundred or more eggs.

Avoid the Itch:
MOSQUITO BITES

The mosquito bite itself is not harmful (although itchy), but mosquitoes sometimes carry germs that can infect humans and other animals. Especially in tropical regions, mosquitoes can carry such serious diseases as malaria or yellow fever and Zika. West Nile encephalitis is a disease that mostly attacks birds, such as crows, but can also affect humans. So it's best to avoid mosquito bites as much as possible. Wear long sleeves and pants if you're in a buggy area, and use nontoxic bug repellent.

Why Me?

Mosquitoes love everything about humans, even our breath. They're attracted to the carbon dioxide we exhale and by our body warmth. But do you ever wonder why mosquitoes seem to like you better than everyone else? It's true that mosquitoes bite some people more than others. That's because everyone has a different scent.

Sniff your own hand. You probably can't smell anything. But every human has a different combination of microbes and bacteria on their body, even after a bath, and these microscopic critters give off a scent. Every person's smell is unique, which is why your dog can sniff you out in a crowd.

Also, mosquitoes are attracted to sweet, flowery odors. So if you use perfume, scented shampoo, or deodorant, you're encouraging mosquitoes to check you out. Mosquitoes like bad smells, too, and they especially love foot odor. When you're camping, if you hang a pair of really smelly socks on a clothesline near your tent, mosquitoes will hover around the socks—and maybe leave you alone.

It's not just humans on the menu—mosquitoes will bite almost anything that breathes: horses and hippos, chickadees and chickens, house cats and mountain lions. The bugs might have a hard time shoving into thick fur or feathers, but they can saw through eyelids or noses. A mosquito might even suck blood from a vampire bat!

Some species of mosquitoes can saw their way into reptile scales to bite rattlesnakes or lizards. If a fish lies in shallow water with a fin sticking out, a mosquito might zero in on it. Mosquitoes are especially fond of biting rats, which have just the right combination of blood proteins for making lots of eggs. To a mother mosquito, the world is just a giant restaurant, filled with meals of protein-rich blood.

Avoid the Itch:
THINK NONTOXIC

When mosquitoes crash the backyard barbeque, it's tempting to reach for a can of chemical bug repellent. But chemicals in bug spray can harm other wildlife, such as birds, butterflies, and frogs, and can affect human health as well. Instead of spraying try these ideas:

- Light a few citronella candles—bugs avoid the smell!

- Plant some catnip—mosquitoes hate catnip scent as much as cats love it.

- Shop for natural bug repellents with herbal ingredients. Read the labels!

Soothe the Itch:
BANANA PEELS

It's hard, but try not to scratch insect bites—scratching only irritates the skin more. If you must scratch, try using a banana instead of your fingernails! Bananas are highly nutritious, and much of the nutrition is contained in the peels, which are full of vitamins, minerals, and antioxidants to help skin heal. Gently rub the inside of the peel on the bite. Ahhhhhhh.

Mosquitoes don't mean to make us itchy. It's just an accident that most humans are allergic to their saliva. But other creatures use the ITCH to send a message loud and clear—and you'd better pay attention!

CHAPTER SIX

TARANTULA!

Remember Me

It's dusk on a lonely Texas highway, with a red summer sun just sinking below the flat horizon. In the distance, a coyote howls.

Then, from the roadside weeds, a strange shape emerges—a bit like a human hand with many moving fingers. In the growing darkness it scuttles across the still-warm blacktop into the grass. Another crawls across the road, and another. If you dare to look closer, you'll see that each is a big spider, with eight legs and two sharp fangs. Each spider is covered with what looks like fuzzy hair.

Beware—the tarantulas are hunting!

There's nothing scarier than a large, hairy spider crawling toward you. But don't worry, tarantulas are not stalking humans—they're hunting tiny prey. Tarantulas eat mostly insects, such as grasshoppers and beetles—not people.

SETAE

But even if they're not looking for you, these furry spiders can cause a big ITCH.

All tarantulas have bristles, called setae, which look like hair. And some species of tarantula have special setae that they use as defense weapons. When threatened, the tarantula will use its back legs to pull setae off its own abdomen. Then it flicks the bristles toward its enemy. The setae are as sharp as slivers of broken glass, and they are incredibly irritating to skin. Many a person who owned a pet tarantula has gotten a faceful of itch as a reward for peering too closely at their pet.

But the tarantula is only trying to irritate you—not kill you. It doesn't want you for food. It just wants to teach you a helpful lesson: Don't get too close!

Think about it. If the tarantula threw poisonous bristles at a predator, such as a coyote, and then the coyote died, that wouldn't really do the spider much good. The tarantula has escaped one predator, true, but there are plenty more out there that are threatening it. And it takes a lot of energy to grow setae—the tarantula doesn't have an unlimited number of prickly weapons to throw.

But the coyote who gets a sore, itchy nose from a tarantula may well remember it and avoid all such creatures in future. And possibly even teach its young to do so as well.

Remember Me— I'm Irritating!

Plants use this strategy too. A plant that makes you itch as soon as you touch it is sending a message: *Don't step on me!* If you ever walked into a patch of nettles, you'd soon stop stomping on the plants. It's different from poison ivy—there's no delayed reaction. You know about the itch right away!

Many plants, such as thistles or cacti, have sharp thorns. But stinging nettles are covered with special structures called urticating hairs. Nettle spines are hollow, and filled with a chemical that's intensely irritating. They squirt a dose of the chemical into your skin, like a doctor using a needle to give you a shot.

Soothe the Itch:
NETTLE RASH

If you wander into a patch of stinging nettles, your skin can sting and itch for hours. Gently rubbing a slice of cool, juicy fruit on your skin can help take away the ouch. Lemons and cucumbers are especially soothing. Onions work too.

Prickly Caterpillars

Some types of caterpillars use the same technique, although most caterpillars are harmless. Out of more than a hundred thousand species of *Lepidoptera* (butterflies and moths) only a few cause itching. But don't get cozy with a tussock moth!

Hickory tussock moths are common caterpillars covered with fuzzy white bristles. They are black and white, like little skunks, and easy to spot on a green leaf. Their bright coloring says *Look at me! I'm bad news!*

Boo!

Because some of those bristles are urticating hairs, like the tarantula's setae or the nettle's spines, and they can cause a nasty rash. The skin on the palm of your hand is fairly thick, so you're unlikely to get a rash from picking up a caterpillar. But if the caterpillar brushes against an area with sensitive skin, such as your arm or your neck, a reaction is more likely.

When a blue jay grabs a caterpillar for lunch, the caterpillar thrashes back and forth, thrusting the urticating hairs into the bird's face. The blue jay quickly learns: *Avoid white, fuzzy food!*

Later, when the caterpillar pupates, it uses the urticating hairs to make its own cocoon. The soft larva inside the cocoon is defenseless, but the cocoon would be an itchy mouthful for hungry predators.

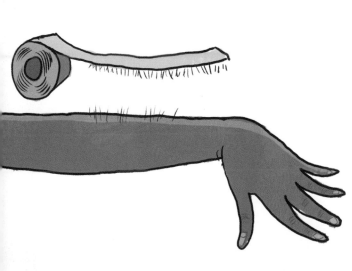

Soothe the Itch:
GET IT ON TAPE

If you feel an itch coming on after handling a caterpillar, don't scratch—that can force the hairs in deeper. Instead, lightly brush your skin with adhesive tape. The fine hairs will stick to the tape and stop bugging you.

Skunked!

You're taking your dog for an evening stroll, and suddenly he darts off into the bushes. In a few minutes he comes back, and you sniff . . . and sniff . . . and then gag at the horrible smell wafting up from your beloved pet. Rover is scratching and whining and rubbing his face in the grass. He's been skunked! And not only does skunk spray smell bad, it's bigtime itchy.

Skunks are small mammals found all over the United States. They're shy, quiet little creatures that potter about in the dusk, digging up worms and insects for food. Seems as if the last thing on their minds is causing trouble. They can't run fast or climb trees, they don't have fangs or claws to fight off predators, but they do have a defense mechanism that's very, very effective.

Skunks are nocturnal animals, mostly active at night. You'd think they'd be all black, so they could hide in the shadows. But skunks have a white stripe—like a warning sign painted down their back—that really stands out in the dark. Just like the tussock moths, skunks want to be noticed.

Skunks can spray a jet of irritating chemicals from their anal glands. The spray is like a jet from a hose. It can travel up to fifteen feet, and their aim is very accurate! The chemicals can cause severe skin irritation that could last for months.

Like tarantulas and tussock moths, skunks aren't aiming to kill their victims. They simply want to send a clear message: *Remember me, or face the consequences.* Next time Rover encounters a small black-and-white animal, he'll run the other way!

Soothe the Itch:
DE-SKUNKING

It's very hard to get rid of skunk odor, but it's important to wash off the skunk spray, for it can cause nasty skin rashes. Douse your pet with vinegar mixed with warm water to rinse off the irritating chemicals—and rinse yourself off, too.

There's something else that can make you itch—something almost invisible. It's not an animal. It's not a plant. There are millions of them, all over the place. But you can't see them coming. You'd need a microscope to spot these teeny-tiny invaders.

45

CHAPTER SEVEN

FUNGUS!

The Invisible Itch

A cheering football team stomps into the locker room after the big game. Shouting and laughing, they're celebrating their championship. They get ready to shower, pulling off heavy shoulder pads and unlacing sweaty shoes.

Each of the players is tall and muscular. They've just defeated another powerful team. But what these athletes don't realize is that underfoot in their locker room is a tiny intruder that can bring them all down.

Spores of fungi, too small to be seen, are lurking on the shower floor.

They're everywhere. There are millions on your skin right now—little dust-like dots of fungus spores. Plants reproduce with seeds, but fungi have spores instead, which can barely be seen with the naked eye. Most aren't the kind that grow on people and are harmless. But there are some species of fungi that feed on human skin.

There are more than a million different species of fungus, in all shapes and sizes, so you might not always recognize it when you see it. Mushrooms are only one kind—fungus can also jut out from dead trees, like a rubbery shelf, or turn bread a disgusting green. Scientists used to classify fungus as a plant, but now we know that in some ways it is more like an animal. Fungus can't make its own food from sun and air, the way plants do. Hungry fungi feed on all sorts of things—dead logs, plant roots, decomposing animals. And some fungi want to feed on you.

The spores of the fungus that cause "athlete's foot" hang out in odd little places we never notice, such as cracks in cement, between shower tiles, or in drains on the locker room floor. If you walk barefoot, some of the spores can get on your skin—and then the fungus starts to grow on you.

Always wear shoes or flip-flops in the locker room and near public showers or pools. And don't wear other people's socks or shoes, especially old sneakers.

Fungus spores need three things in order to grow: darkness, moisture, and warmth. So a sweaty foot in a damp sneaker is a perfect habitat. Since athletes often wear sweaty sneakers and hang out in locker rooms, the fungus is known as athlete's foot, although anyone with damp feet can get it—swimmers, dancers, hikers.

The athlete's foot fungus devours a protein called keratin, which is found all over your body, especially in hair, nails, and skin. But fungus doesn't have a mouth, or a stomach—so how does it eat?

You eat food, then digest it inside your stomach. A fungus digests the food before eating it. The fungus gives off acids and enzymes, digestive chemicals that break particles of dead skin down into simple molecules. Then the fungus absorbs the nutrients through a network of threads called hyphae, which are like the roots of a tiny tree. It's the digestive enzymes dissolving your skin that make you itchy.

Athlete's foot isn't usually a serious health threat. In fact, at first you might not even notice it. But after a while your skin gets irritated by the fungus's annoying habit of digesting its meals between your toes. The skin gets rough and dry, peels, and can be seriously itchy.

Soothe the Itch:

YOUR FEET IN THE SUN

If you do get athlete's foot, deny the fungus the darkness and moisture it needs. Keep your feet in the light—wear sandals when possible. Always dry your feet well, and change shoes and socks when they're damp.

A sprinkling of foot powder over your toes and in your shoes can help keep feet cozy and dry.

Ugh! No one wants fungus on their skin! Seems like it would be great if we could get rid of all the fungi in the world. But as gross as they are, we need them—they're the planet's garbage collectors. Most types of fungi are decomposers—they eat dead things and help break them down into soil. A world without fungi would be no fun.

Seems as though itch-causing things are everywhere! And one of the itchiest creatures of all could be lurking under your bed . . .

FOOT POWDER

CHAPTER EIGHT

BEDBUGS!

Learning a Smelly Language

Awoman holds a glass jar filled with hundreds of tiny crawling insects. Removing the lid, she presses the open mouth of the jar against her arm. The insects rush to bite her skin, each one draining a drop of her blood with their sharp, sucking mouthparts. She watches as they feast. When all the bugs have satisfied their hunger, she replaces the lid and opens the next jar.

It's just another day in the lab for Dr. Regine Gries, an entomologist and bedbug expert. Over the course of her five-year research, she's allowed herself to be bitten by bedbugs more than 180,000 times.

Bedbugs love darkness. By day, the brown, wingless bugs cluster together, hidden under mattresses, in pillowcases, and between blankets. At night they creep out to bite their sleeping human host.

Dr. Regine Gries is a biologist at Simon Fraser University in Vancouver, Canada. Dr. Gries and her coworkers, Dr. Gerhard Gries and Dr. Robert Britton, have spent years studying bedbugs. They needed to experiment with a large colony of hungry bugs, so Dr. Gries volunteered to be their food, as she happens to be immune to bedbug bites. Her arms have fed more than a thousand bugs each week for five years.

Like fleas and lice, bedbugs feast on blood. Bedbug bites can cause intense itching, skin sores, and rashes, and they may also carry diseases. No one wants to share a bed with these irritating bugs, but it's incredibly difficult to get rid of them.

During the day, their flat bodies squeeze into the tiniest cracks and seams. You might be able to find most of the bedbugs in a bed, but it's impossible to find them all, and if even one female survives, she can lay hundreds of eggs. Bedbugs can live up to a year without eating and can survive freezing temperatures for days.

Soothe the Itch:
MINTY FRESHNESS

Toothpaste, especially the kind that's mint-flavored, is cool and soothing to itchy bug bites. It keeps the irritated skin clean and helps reduce swelling, too. Just dab a little toothpaste on the bite and let it dry. Rinse and repeat as needed.

In the twentieth century, it seemed that scientists had found a weapon that could exterminate bedbugs: the newly invented miracle pesticide called DDT. However, it turned out that DDT posed serious health risks for people and also harmed birds and other wildlife. DDT was banned for use in the United States in 1972.

It's difficult to exterminate bedbugs with pesticides. These bugs are tough, and they quickly develop resistance to poisons. The strongest of them survive and lay eggs, creating more and more pesticide-resistant offspring.

Chemicals powerful enough to wipe out a bedbug infestation may be bad for people, too. No one wants to sleep on a pesticide-soaked mattress. No doubt about it, getting rid of bedbugs is a challenge!

Avoid the Itch:
NOWHERE TO HIDE

Bedbugs like to hide in places that are quiet, dark, and undisturbed. So shake things up! Turn your mattress over every now and then. Frequently shake out your quilts and blankets, or hang bedding on a sunny clothesline.

Dr. Gries and her partners have studied bedbugs, trying to find a solution. They noticed that the bugs would often cluster together in groups. How did the bedbugs find each other in the dark?

Scientists have long known that many insects, including bedbugs, "talk" to each other with smells. The bugs release chemicals, called pheromones, in the air. Humans can't smell them, but the chemicals send a clear message to insects.

So Dr. Gries and her partners began to learn the bedbugs' smelly language.

They discovered that some pheromones mean *Something good to eat over here.* Other odors say *Danger!* And when a bedbug finds a dark, cozy place to hide, it gives off a scented signal that means *Come here—safe shelter!*

The "safe shelter" pheromone doesn't harm humans, but it's irresistible to bedbugs, and it's cheap and easy to make in the laboratory. Using this smelly message as bait, scientists may be able to create the perfect trap for bedbugs. No more need for toxic sprays or expensive visits from the exterminator. If the bedbug trap works, it could solve an itchy problem that has plagued humans for millennia.

Itching can be one of the most annoying sensations on earth. But there are some things worse than being itchy. In fact, some people might say, better ITCH than OUCH!

CHAPTER NINE

ITCHING?

Is There Anything Good About Itching?

Salem, Massachusetts, 1630

The old woman had long been known far and wide as a witch. Her neighbors whispered that she had magical powers. Why, she used all kinds of strange ingredients—nettles, fungus, poison ivy—to make brews in her cauldron. But her cures were often surprisingly successful, which only fueled the rumors that she could work magic.

This time her patient was an old man who had long been suffering from sore, stiff joints. Sometimes the pain was so bad he could barely move. The woman approached her patient carrying a handful of stinging nettles. Muttering a spell, she rubbed them on his sore knees and elbows.

Ow! Ouch! The patient's skin itched and burned. But soon a grin spread across his face—because suddenly the pain was much less.

Magic?

Stinging nettles—some of the prickliest, itchiest plants in the world—have been used for thousands of years as a remedy for sore and aching joints. The herbalists who used plants as remedies were often feared as witches, but sometimes their strange remedies worked for sound scientific reasons.

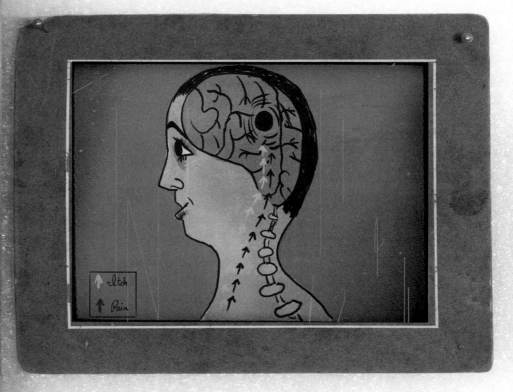

Your brain processes the sensation of itching differently from that of pain. Scientists used to think that itching was just a milder form of pain, but neuro-scientists have discovered that itching is different from other kinds of touch or temperature sensations. Scientists now believe that although itch and pain may share some nerve receptors, they send messages to the brain by different pathways.

By rubbing nettles on a painful joint, a new sensation—ITCH—overrides the constant message of OUCH OUCH OUCH that is flowing along the nerves to the brain. Nettles can be used as a kind of medication known as a counterirritant. The stinging and tingling caused by the nettles diverts the brain's attention from other feelings. A brisk massage of stinging nettles can dramatically relieve pain for many hours.

Avoid the Itch:
DON'T TRY THIS AT HOME!

Counterirritant medications should be used under the supervision of a doctor, so don't try rubbing nettles on yourself!

The liquid inside the nettle's urticating hairs contains histamine, which is a chemical that makes blood vessels widen. This extra flow of blood makes the skin feel warm. In fact, long ago, people suffering from cold would flog themselves with nettles, figuring that even a burning itch was better than freezing. The extra blood also helps heal wounds and sores.

So, okay, maybe itching can be better than hurting. But wouldn't it be great not to feel any of those annoying sensations at all?

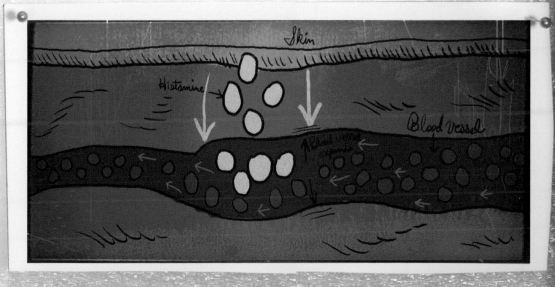

A Good Scratch

Every time you feel an itch, it's an opportunity. You have a chance to notice that something is amiss. The itch may be annoying, but it's better than not realizing that you have a problem. Think of each itch as an alarm clock that says *Pay attention!*

For example, you probably don't spend too much time looking at your toes. Itchiness tells you that perhaps fungus has invaded. Or, as you reach to scratch your head, you might notice a little bug scuttling away. In a way, it's a good thing that louse bites are itchy. The bites themselves don't hurt, and if it weren't for the itch, you might never know you were hosting lice!

An itchy skin makes birds take a dirt bath. Particles of dust and sand rub off parasites that could cause health problems. Itchiness makes a bear rub his back against a tree. This soothes the itch, but it also rubs off shedding fur, leaving his coat clean and shiny.

A Good Itch?

Itch-causers such as lice, fleas, bedbugs, mosquitoes, and fungi do unpleasant things—suck blood, cause sores, even give us diseases. Seems as though nothing could be worse than these maddening parasites.

Parasites need their hosts in order to survive. But in recent years some scientists have begun to ask a really weird question. Some parasites need humans, yes—but what if humans need some parasites?

The Hygiene Hypothesis

Hygiene means cleanliness, and clean is good, right? Wouldn't it be great if we lived in a sparkling clean world—no fleas, lice, cacti, or fungi, no disgusting bedbugs or annoying mosquitoes—where nothing ever made us itchy or sick? But there's a possibility that irritating things can actually make us healthier.

For millions of years humans have fought to survive parasites, fungi, and germs. So our bodies' immune systems evolved to cope with all those things.

But over the centuries, we've cleaned things up a lot.

In 1999 a Swiss doctor named Charlotte Braun-Fahrländer noticed something odd. Kids who lived on farms, in close contact with manure, bugs, fungi, and germs, were often surprisingly healthy. In fact, they tended to be healthier than kids who grew up in very clean houses and rarely touched animals or messed around in the mud.

Dr. Braun-Fahrländer and many other scientists are studying the "hygiene hypothesis," which says that living in an environment free of germs, dirt, and parasites makes us weaker, not stronger.

When a parasite or an infection attacks your body, your immune system fights back. It could be that battling parasites helps your immune system develop and strengthen, so that it's better able to protect you.

Fighting the Wrong Enemy

Our immune systems have developed to fight off a constant barrage of germs and parasites. When there aren't any "bad guys" to fight, the immune system doesn't just shut down. It searches for something to battle, and sometimes it chooses a harmless thing—like mosquito spit. Or louse saliva, or poison ivy sap, or bedbug nibbles. Your immune system overreacts to these harmless things, making you sneeze, cough, or itch. People who grow up in environments that are very clean tend to have nastier reactions to bug bites and poison ivy, to sneeze more when it's pollen season, and to have more allergies.

So putting up with some irritating plants, animals, and fungi might be worth it if they can help our immune systems work properly. Fighting the itch could even help protect us against serious diseases, such as multiple sclerosis or diabetes, which are caused by an overactive immune system.

Strange as it seems, our bodies don't work as well if everything around us is too clean and perfect. Maybe we need a little bit of ITCH!

Author's Note

I got interested in the topic of *Itch!* when I discovered my grandfather's journal, hidden in a long-forgotten box in the attic. He was a soldier in World War I, and it was amazing to read his words, scribbled in pencil each day of that terrible war. I was surprised to find that even as he was dodging sniper bullets, one of the main problems on his mind was being itchy.

Lice were a constant torment, and he called the hated bugs "cooties." He was thrilled when he finally got to do what he'd been dreaming of for many months: take a bath. He wrote "I AM COOTIE-LESS!!!" in giant letters across the page.

I started to wonder how such tiny critters could produce such a big effect on people—and why.

Glossary

ALLERGEN: A substance causing an allergic reaction that can lead to symptoms such as itching.

ANTICOAGULANT: A chemical that prevents blood from thickening.

DERMIS: The middle layer of the skin, containing blood vessels, sweat glands, and nerves.

EPIDERMIS: The outer layer of the skin.

EXOSKELETON: The hard outer coating of an insect.

GLOCHIDS: Barbed spines or bristles that can easily detach from a plant and cause an allergic itch.

HERBICIDE: A chemical that can kill plants.

HISTAMINE: A chemical that can cause blood vessels to swell and causes many symptoms of allergic reaction.

HYGIENE: Cleanliness.

HYPODERMIS: The innermost layer of the skin, mostly made up of fatty tissue.

IMMUNE SYSTEM: A complex network of cells and tissues that protect the body from germs and other threats.

PESTICIDE: A chemical that can kill plants and animals.

PHEROMONE: A chemical an animal produces in its body, which affects the behavior of other members of the same species.

RESILIN: A rubbery, stretchy protein found in insect legs and wings.

SETAE: Stiff hairs or bristles on plants or animals.

URUSHIOL: An oily liquid found in poison ivy and other plants, which causes an itchy allergic reaction in many (but not all) humans.

Notes

11 "arithmetic bugs . . . multiplied!": W. A. Carter, quoted in Asprey, *At Belleau Wood*.

17 "You won't . . . amazement!": Adam Gertsacov, quoted in Martin, "Old-Time Vaudeville Looks Young Again."

19 "Insect jumping . . . be fantastic.": Gregory Sutton, quoted in Morgan, "The Secret of the Flea's Famous Jump."

Bibliography

Asprey, Robert. *At Belleau Wood.* Denton: University of North Texas Press, 1996.

Baerg, William. *The Tarantula.* Ithaca, N.Y.: Cornell University Press, 1958.

Burdick, Alan. *Out of Eden: An Odyssey of Ecological Invasion.* New York: Farrar, Straus, and Giroux, 2005.

Burkett-Cadena, Nathan. *Mosquitoes of the Southeastern United States.* Tuscaloosa: University of Alabama Press, 2013.

Diamond, Jared. *Guns, Germs, and Steel: The Fate of Human Societies.* New York: W. W. Norton, 2005.

Epstein, William L. "Allergic Contact Dermatitis." *Current Perspectives in Immunodermatology.* London: Churchill Livingstone Publishers, 1984.

Erichsen-Brown, Charlotte. *Medicinal and Other Uses of North American Plants.* New York: Dover Publications, 1979.

Foster, Steven, and Rebecca L. Johnson. *National Geographic Desk Reference to Nature's Medicine.* National Geographic Society, 2006.

Gullen, P. J., and P. S. Cranston. *The Insects: An Outline of Entomology.* Hoboken, N.J.: Blackwell Publishing, 2010.

Habif, Thomas P., James L. Campbell, Shane Chapman, and James G. Dinulo. *Skin Disease: Diagnosis and Treatment.* Maryland Heights, Mo.: C. V. Mosby, 2011.

James, Maurice, and Robert Harwood. *Medical Entomology.* New York: Macmillan, 1969.

Lewallen, Robin, Adele Clark, and Steven Feldman. *Clinical Handbook of Contact Dermatitis: Diagnosis and Management.* Boca Raton, Fla.: CRC Press, 2014.

Marshall, Samuel D. *Tarantulas and Other Arachnids.* Barron Educational Series, 2001.

Martin, Douglas. "Old-Time Vaudeville Looks Young Again." *New York Times,* November 24, 2002. (www.nytimes.com.)

Moerman, Daniel. *Native American Food Plants: An Ethnobotanical Dictionary.* Portland, Ore.: Timber Press, 2010.

Morgan, Patrick. "The Secret of the Flea's Famous Jump." *Discover: Science for the Curious.* February 10, 2011. (www.discovermagazine.com.)

Niethammer, Carolyn, and Robin Stancliff. *The Prickly Pear Cookbook.* Tucson, Ariz.: Rio Nuevo Publishers, 2004.

Persico, Joseph. *Eleventh Month, Eleventh Day, Eleventh Hour: Armistice Day, 1918.* New York: Random House, 2004.

Petersen, Jens. *The Kingdom of Fungi.* Princeton, N.J.: Princeton University Press, 2013.

Piffard, Henry G. *A Treatise on the Materia Medica and Therapeutics of the Skin.* New York: William Wood & Company, 1881.

Spielman, Andrew, and Michael D'Antonio. *Mosquito: The Story of Man's Deadliest Foe.* New York: Hachette Book Group, 2002.

Stewart, Amy. *Wicked Bugs.* Chapel Hill, N.C.: Algonquin Books, 2011.

Velasquez-Manoff, Moises. *An Epidemic of Absence: A New Way of Understanding Allergies and Autoimmune Diseases.* New York: Simon and Schuster, 2012.

Wagner, David. *Caterpillars of Eastern North America.* Princeton, N.J.: Princeton University Press, 2005.

Zinsser, Hans. *Rats, Lice, and History.* Piscataway, N.J.: Transaction Publications, 2007. First published in 1935.

Websites

American Academy of Dermatology: www.aad.org

Arthritis Research UK: www.arthritisresearchuk.org

Center for the Study of Itch at Washington University: csi.wustl.edu

Johns Hopkins Medical Library: www.hopkinsmedicine.org/healthlibrary/conditions/dermatology

Mayo Clinic: www.mayoclinic.org/diseases-conditions

National Geographic Society, "How Do Fleas Jump?": news.nationalgeographic.com/news/2011/02/110211-fleas-jump-mystery-science-animals (includes video)

National Science Teachers Association: www.nsta.org/?utm_source=RealMagnet&utm_medium=e-mail&utm_campaign=SciClassElem

New York State Department of Environmental Conservation, "Integrated Pest Management In and Around Your Home": www.dec.ny.gov/docs/materials_minerals_pdf/pm2.pdf

U.S. Center for Disease Control and Prevention: www.cdc.gov

Index

Index *(continued)*